D1398269

D Is For Dinosaur

A Rhyme Book and More

by

Ken and Mally Ham

Master Books

D IS FOR DINOSAUR
A RHYME BOOK AND MORE

First printing: 1991
Eleventh printing: October 2001

Master Books
P.O. Box 727
Green Forest, AR 72638

ISBN: 0-89051-193-4
Library of Congress Number: 91-72184

Color and black and white illustrations by Ron Hight
Illustration concepts by Ken Ham and Ron Hight

Printed in China

Please visit our website for other great titles:
www.masterbooks.net

Instructions
On How To Use
This Multipurpose Family Book

---

1. Entertaining ABC Rhyme Book

Children and parents alike will enjoy the colorful and oftentimes humorous pictures on each page of this book. The first section can be used either by parents to read to their young children, or else children can read it for themselves. It will not only take them through the alphabet, but they will also learn about Biblical creation, dinosaurs, and salvation.

As you read each rhyme and comment on the pictures, encourage the children to remember the concepts that will help them defend the Bible, and reject evolutionary ideas.

2. Coloring Book

In the second part of the book, black and white drawings of the color pictures are included so that children can either color them in with their own color schemes, or copy the colors in the first section of the book. This will help reinforce the Biblical concepts they learned as they read through the first part of the book.

3. Sunday School/Christian School/Home School/Home Devotional Teaching Book

The second part of the book contains notes for parents and teachers, along with student exercises which will enable children to go step-by-step through the concepts portrayed on each page.

This book could also be used as a text for teaching the alphabet, as well as many things about science and the Bible, with an emphasis on dinosaurs, creation, and the flood. The Gospel message is clearly presented, and an opportunity for commitment is given.

It is suggested that the black and white pictures be photocopied and handed out to each student, either to color in or just to keep as part of the lesson.

For teaching purposes, these black and white pictures could also be made into overhead transparencies, using a photocopier. Color could be added by using either water-based or oil-based overhead transparency pens, or something similar.

We are praying that you will enjoy using this book as much as we have enjoyed writing and designing it.

We sincerely thank everyone who contributed suggestions as we put this publication together, especially Joy Rizor for her editorial skills, and Ron Hight for his God-given artistic ability. We also thank Mary Nulton, Marge Appelquist, Dr. John Morris, and Dr. Henry Morris for their valuable insights, and Don Rohrer for his administrative abilities in arranging the publishing aspects. This book is dedicated to our five children, Nathan, Renee, Danielle, Jeremy, and Kristel, who love to read books — especially God's Word.

A B C D E F G

God made the world, it's plain to see.

HIJKLMN

But did He make dinosaurs, and if so, when?

———————————————

OPQR
STU

The Bible has the answer,
God's Word is true.

V W X Y and Z

We'll learn the truth about history.

A is for **Answers** from God's Holy Book;
Just open the pages and take a good look.
God created the earth, in space it did hang;
Creation's first day, without a BIG BANG.

B is for **Bible**, where it says on day two,
God made the clean air for me and for you.
He divided the waters above and below;
Day three comes next, so there we shall go.

C is for **Continent**, the first dry land,
Which God raised up by His powerful hand.
Then He commanded that all the plants grow;
The third day was truly a beautiful show.

15

Dis for **Dinosaur**, but you'll have to wait,
'Cause on day four other things God did make.
He formed the sun, the stars, and the moon.
Are you ready? We'll see those dinosaurs soon!

E is for **Everything** that swims in the seas,
Made on day five, with the birds in the trees.
He also created the great Plesiosaur;
Reading God's Word, we can know this for sure.

_____

F is for **Fantastic** - that's all we can say,
As we see what God made on this, the sixth day!
Adam and Eve and the pouched kangaroo;
The rest of the animals and dinosaurs, too.

G is for the **Garden** God specially made,
Where Adam and Eve could always have stayed.
Living in Eden, a world without sin;
What a beautiful place for them to live in.

23

H is for **Hungry,** it's how we describe
A big dinosaur with his mouth open wide.
Adam wasn't scared to watch dinosaurs eat,
Because all the creatures ate plants, and not meat.

I is the letter in the middle of sIn,
To remind us all of the trouble we're in.
Dinosaurs, people, and the whole universe;
Because of man's sin, God judged with a curse.

Tree Of Knowledge Of Good and Evil

6-DAY CHRONICLE

Adam Sins...
World in Chaos

J means **Just** awful - I'm sure we could say
The effects of sin grew worse every day.
Flesh became violent, the Bible reveals.
Were people and creatures now dinosaur meals?

———————————————————

29

**K** is for **Knowledge,** which made Noah sad;
The world would be judged,
because people were bad!
God warned He would send a terrible flood
That would cover the world with water and mud.

L is for **Listen**: Noah knew that he should,
As soon as God said, "Make an ark out of wood.
Take each land animal, two by two;
Your family will be the hard-working crew."

———————————————————

**M** is for **Monster** like the great dinosaur;
But how could he enter the ark through the door?
Well, many dinosaurs were really quite small;
The young ones, especially, were not very tall.

N is for **Noah**, his wife, and his kin,
Who, with the animals, also went in.
Dinosaurs outside the ark were all drowned;
That's why as fossils their bones are now found.

O is for **Out** of the ark they all ran,
  Once the huge vessel came safely to land.
Stegasaurs, lambeosaurs, nodosaurs and more;
After the flood there were dinosaurs galore!

P is for **Pronounce**: are the names hard for you?
Iguanodon, diplodocus, now how did you do?
Brachiosaurus, tyrannosaurus, and others as well,
What happened to them is the story we'll tell.

———————————————————————

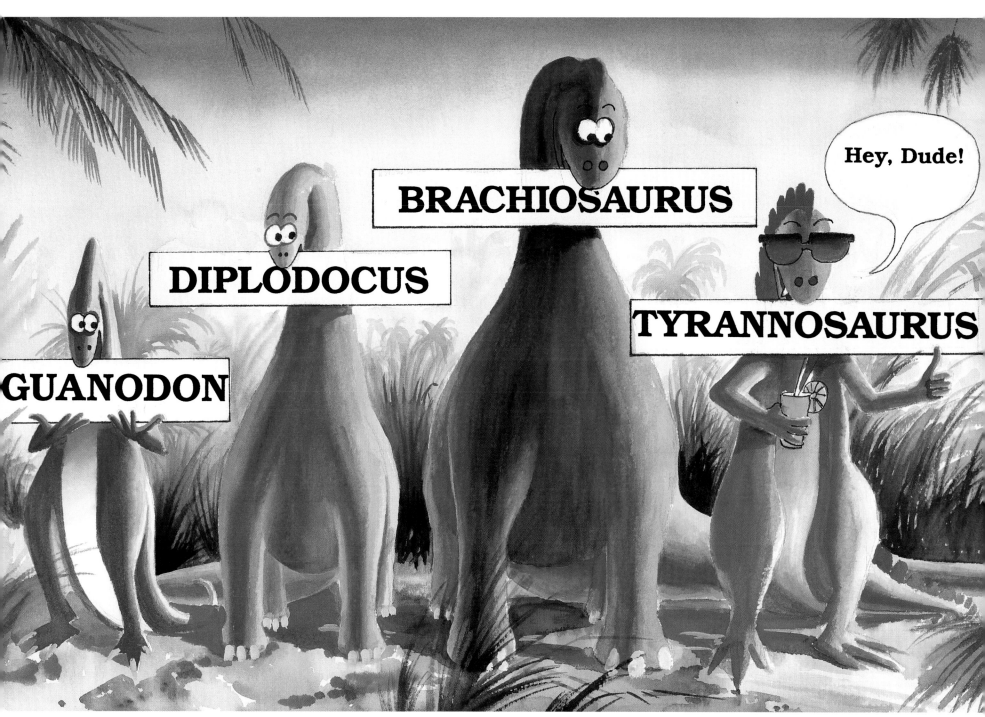

41

Q is for **Question** - why can't we any more,
Look around and see even one dinosaur?
They're surely all dead, it's as simple as that;
Try to guess why - put on your thinking hat.

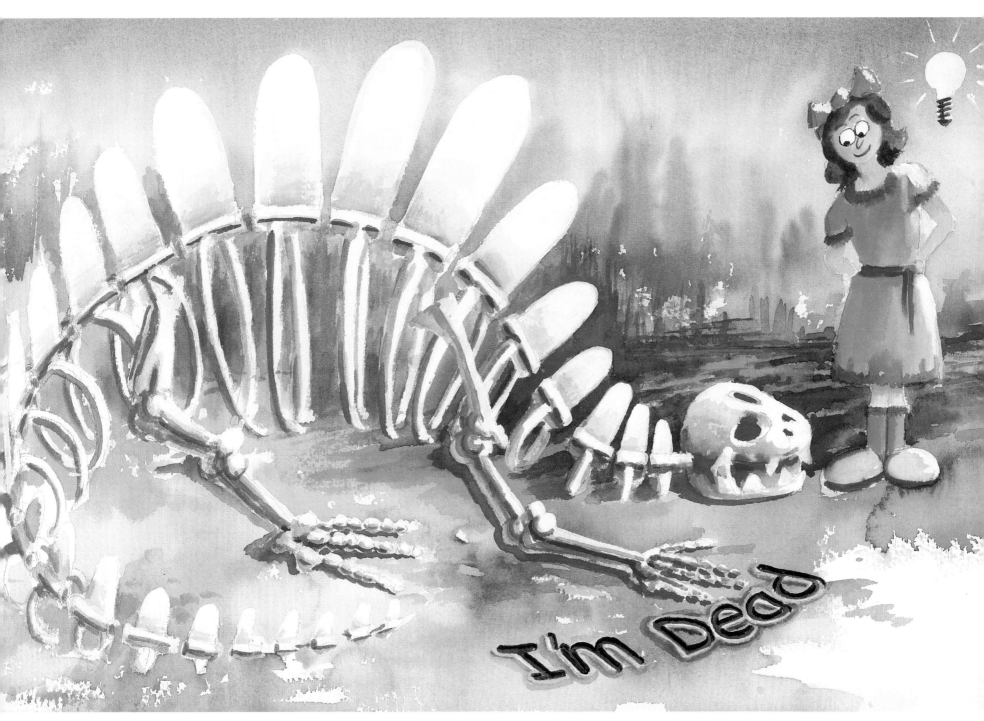

43

R is for **Reasons** - perhaps there are more.
After the flood, times were tougher for sure:
Volcanoes and storms, then drought and snow,
Maybe people killed them -
they frightened them so.

S is for the **Story** from God's Holy Book;
About a great beast;
when he walked the ground shook.
Behemoth, or monster, was this animal's name;
Our word "dinosaur" means almost the same.

T is for **Tales** that we often hear
About terrible dragons that made men fear.
Maybe these tales could actually be
Stories of dinosaurs men used to see.

U is for **Understand**, which we want to do;
The Bible explains the dinosaurs for you.
It also tells how from sin to be saved;
By trusting in Jesus, who rose from the grave.

51

V is for how **Very** much we can say
We all should read the Bible each day.
Dinosaurs, we've proven, are no mystery;
God's Word teaches us true history.

53

W is for **Watchfulness**
which we should all learn,
Since some day Jesus, our Lord, will return.
He's going to judge this world once again;
But this time by fire, instead of by rain.

The
BIG BANG
is
definitely
coming!

DYNAMITE

is in e**X**cited, which Christians should be,
One day we know that heaven we'll see.
There'll be no more dying, or crying or pain;
For God our Creator, forever will reign.

57

Y is for **Years**, how long could it be,
Since God made the world for you and for me?
"Probably only six thousand or so,"
Say many good scientists; they ought to know!

_____

Z is for the **Zeal** which people should see,
As we tell the truth about history.
The dinosaurs certainly have not evolved;
Through God's Holy Word, the puzzle is solved!

_____

61

Draw your favorite dinosaur here

Section 2

Student coloring book section
and parent/teacher notes

Genesis I

The creation

In the beginning God created the heaven and the earth.

2 And the earth was without form, and void; and darkness *was* upon the face of the deep. And the Spirit of God moved upon the face of the waters.

First day: light

3 And God said, Let there be light: and there was light.

4 And God saw the light, that *it was* good: and God divided the light from the darkness.

5 And God called the light Day, and the darkness he called Night. And the evening and the morning were the first day.

Second day: firmament

6 And God said, Let there be a firmament in the midst of the waters, and let it divide the waters from the waters.

7 And God made the firmament, and divided the waters which *were* under the firmament from the waters which *were* above the firmament: and it was so.

8 And God called the firmament Heaven. And the evening and the morning were the second day.

Third day: seas, land, and vegetation

9 And God said, Let the waters under the heaven be gathered together unto one place, and let the dry *land* appear: and it was so.

10 And God called the dry *land* Earth; and the gathering together of the waters called he Seas: and God saw that *it was* good.

11 And God said, Let the earth bring forth grass, the herb yielding seed, *and* the fruit tree yielding fruit after his kind, whose seed *is* in itself, upon the earth: and it was so.

12 And the earth brought forth grass, *and* herb yielding seed after his kind, and the tree yielding fruit, whose seed *was* in itself, after his kind: and God saw that *it was* good.

13 And the evening and the morning were the third day.

Fourth day: heavenly bodies

14 And God said, Let there be lights in the firmament of the heaven to divide the day from the night; and let them be for signs, and for seasons, and for days, and years:

15 And let them be for lights in the firmament of the heaven to give light upon the earth: and it was so.

16 And God made two great lights; the greater light to rule the day, and the lesser light to rule the night: *he made* the stars also.

17 And God set them in the firmanent of the heaven to give light upon the earth,
18 And to rule over the day and over the night, and to divide the light from the darkness: and God saw that *it was* good.
19 And the evening and the morning were the fourth day.

Fifth day: animal life of sea and air

20 And God said, Let the waters bring forth abundantly the moving creature that hath life, and fowl *that* may fly above the earth in the open firmament of heaven.
21 And God created great whales, and every living creature that moveth, which the waters brought forth abundantly, after their kind, and every winged fowl after his kind: and God saw that *it was* good.
22 And God blessed them, saying, Be fruitful, and multiply, and fill the waters in the seas, and let fowl multiply in the earth.
23 And the evening and the morning were the fifth day.

Sixth day: (1) animal life of earth

24 And God said, Let the earth bring forth the living creature after his kind, cattle, and creeping thing, and beast of the earth after his kind: and it was so.
25 And God made the beast of the earth after his kind, and cattle after their kind, and every thing that creepeth upon the earth after his kind: and God saw that *it was* good.

Sixth day: (2) man

26 And God said, Let us make man in our image, after our likeness: and let them have dominion over the fish of the sea, and over the fowl of the air, and over the cattle, and over all the earth, and over every creeping thing that creepeth upon the earth.
27 So God created man in his *own* image, in the image of God created he him; male and female created he them.
28 And God blessed them, and God said unto them, Be fruitful, and multiply, and replenish the earth, and subdue it: and have dominion over the fish of the sea, and over the fowl of the air, and over every living thing that moveth upon the earth.

Provision of food

29 And God said, Behold, I have given you every herb bearing seed, which *is* upon the face of all the earth, and every tree, in the which *is* the fruit of a tree yielding seed; to you it shall be for meat.
30 And to every beast of the earth, and to every fowl of the air, and to every thing that creepeth upon the earth, wherein *there is* life, *I have given* every green herb for meat: and it was so.
31 And God saw every thing that he had made, and, behold, *it was* very good. And the evening and the morning were the sixth day.

ABCDEFG

God made the world, it's plain to see.

Notes For Parents and Teachers

Carefully read through Genesis Chapter 1 with the children before you teach the following sections. It would be a good idea to reread this chapter several times as you teach these exercises.

Some of the exercises may be too difficult for some students, depending upon their age level, etc. However, teachers can modify and adapt the ideas to teach the concepts.

"For the invisible things of him from the creation of the world are clearly seen, being understood by the things that are made, even his eternal power and Godhead; so that they are without excuse:" (Romans 1:20). This verse points out that there is overwhelming evidence that God created, and that if people don't believe it, they are without excuse. This evidence is clearly seen all around us, because functional complexity (e.g., a functioning machine) can never be developed from disorder, by chance. To explain this to young children, you can use examples such as the following:

1. Show them a picture of Mount Rushmore, and make it clear to them that the Presidents' heads did not get there from millions of years of wind and water erosion, but by people who applied intelligence to make the carvings.

2. Point out that airplanes and watches and computers don't come together by chance — they have been designed and made by people.

3. Show them a pebble out of a stream, and an Indian arrowhead. Ask them to pick out the arrowhead. Discuss why they made their choice, explaining that it is easy to recognize something that has been designed.

By using these examples you can show them that life, which is much more complicated than a computer or an airplane, also had to be made by someone — God. Life could not have happened by chance. Through these examples, you can reinforce the whole concept of recognizing the evidence of intelligence. Repeat the above examples, emphasizing the fact that it is easy to recognize the effect of intelligence, and thus it is easy to recognize that there is a Creator, because of all there is around us. It is plain to see that God made the world.

Student Exercise

Put a number of Lego bricks (about 100) into a shoe box, place the lid on the box, and have the children shake the box and then look at the result. Repeat this five times, then have the children build a house out of the Lego bricks. Explain the difference between chance and intelligence to produce order.

HIJK LMN

But did He make dinosaurs, and if so, when?

Notes For Parents and Teachers

Most children, particularly those from Christian homes, have no difficulty recognizing that God made the different animals and plants. However, because of the intensive evolutionary indoctrination through television, the public education system, books, etc., most children do not think of God as having made the dinosaurs. They tend to think of dinosaurs as primitive creatures that lived long before man, and that they really have nothing to do with creation.

The topic of dinosaurs is probably used more than anything else to convince young people that evolution is true, and that the process took millions of years. Explain to them why it is obvious that God had to make life, and since dinosaurs were living creatures, then obviously God had to make them too — they couldn't have happened just by mere chance. Colossians 1:16 states, "All things were created by him, and for him." The "All" must include dinosaurs that once existed on the earth.

Often the term "prehistoric" is used in reference to animals like dinosaurs. The term "prehistoric" means before recorded history — long before man; however, (and this will be obvious in other sections of the book) the Bible is a record of history since time began, and the Bible says man was created on day six along with the land animals. (Genesis 1: 24-31).

Student Exercise

Have the children draw their favorite dinosaur. Emphasize how hard it is just to draw a dinosaur — let alone make one. If it takes a lot of intelligence to draw a dinosaur, it must have taken MUCH MORE intelligence to make one in the first place.

OPQ
RSTU

The Bible has the answer, God's Word is true.

Notes For Parents and Teachers

The Bible tells us in Colossians that in Christ "are hid all the treasures of wisdom and knowledge" (Colossians 2:3). This means that only God knows everything, and only God **always** tells the truth (John 17:17).

It is important to get across to the children that, compared to what God knows, what any human knows is almost nothing. Therefore, if we are going to find out the truth about the dinosaurs, or how the world came into existence, or how anything ever got here at all, we need to consult the one who knows everything. Stress to them that no scientist knows everything, but that the Bible tells us God knows everything, so we should go to the Bible to find the answers.

Student Exercise

Have the children use an ink pen to draw a very small dot on a blank page. Then get them to take another blank page, and start making dots all over the page. They can continue doing this for a couple of minutes. Explain to them that the one dot on the page represents how much man knows, but all the other dots they have drawn on the other page are just a start in representing what God knows. Tell them that they could continue making dots FOREVER — and God would still know MUCH more than that. Help them to begin to understand what it means that God has infinite knowledge.

V W X Y and Z

We'll learn the truth about history.

Notes For Parents and Teachers

Look up Job 38:4. Here God asked Job the question, "Where wast thou when I laid the foundations of the earth?" In other words, teach the children that God was really asking Job, "Were you there?"

Share with them that not only does God know everything, but He has always been there. The only way we can know what happened to the dinosaurs, for instance, is to talk to someone who knows everything, who's always been there. Tell them that only God knows everything and has always been there, and that we should go to His Word to understand this world, and even to look for clues regarding dinosaurs.

Also share with them that the next time a teacher (or anyone) talks about "millions of years ago," the student could ask, "Were you there?" Explain that no human being knows everything, or has always been there, so how can they really know what happened in the past?

Student Exercise

Give each student an M&M to eat. Have some of them go outside and eat it without anyone watching. Then ask each student to prove they ate an M&M. It should be obvious that those who have witnesses will have an easier time attempting to prove this than those without witnesses. However, also discuss the fact that the witnesses have to

be reliable, and they may not have observed carefully enough — maybe some witnesses didn't tell the truth. Some may use evidence such as chocolate around the mouth, or on the tongue, to "prove" they ate an M&M. But this could also be interpreted as having been an ordinary piece of chocolate — not an M&M. Actually, in the final analysis, they can't PROVE they ate an M&M, because it happened in the past. Explain how much easier it is to substantiate a fact when there are witnesses.

If you want to give the students a more difficult question — ask them to prove the color of the M&M they ate! In order to "prove" this, they would have had to specifically show it to someone before they ate it.

A is for **Answers** from God's Holy Book;
Just open the pages and take a good look.
God created the earth, in space it did hang;
Creation's first day, without a BIG BANG.

Notes For Parents and Teachers

God tells us in the book of Genesis that when He made the earth it was covered with water (Genesis 1:2; II Peter 3:5). The Bible also says that the sun was not created until day four, which is totally the opposite of evolutionary teaching (Genesis 1:14-19).

Much of modern science tells us that the universe began with a "Big Bang" billions of years ago, that the sun came before the earth, and that, eventually, the earth was formed as a hot molten blob. Show that this contradicts what the Bible says.

If the earth were created first, and covered with water, then there never was a "Big Bang." Teach the children that in II Peter 3, God tells us what will happen in the last days, when this earth, as we know it, will finally be judged by fire and changed back into a perfect world. We read in II Peter 3:10, that when the earth is judged by fire, the elements will melt with great heat, and that there will be a great noise. Explain to them that this means there will be a "Big Bang" in the future, but that there never was a "Big Bang" in the past!

You can also share with the children that the Bible teaches explicitly that the earth hung in space — it does not sit on pillars, or anything similar to pillars (Job 26:7). Also, it is not flat (Proverbs 8:27; Isaiah 40:22). Share with them that people in the past thought the earth was flat, but if they had read the Bible, they would have had a scientifically correct understanding of the earth.

Again emphasize to them the importance of reading God's Word in order to understand the correct teaching about the earth.

Student Exercise

On one side of a sheet of paper, have the students write the following, one underneath the other: "Big Bang," sun before earth, earth a hot molten blob, no water on the earth at first, happened over billions of years. Now ask the students to write on the other side what the Bible tells us concerning these matters. They can attempt this on their own by using Genesis Chapter 1: No "Big Bang," earth before sun, earth cool (because it was covered with water), earth covered with water, creation finished in six days. Emphasize that the order of events according to the Bible is totally different from the theory of evolution. Stress the importance of trusting God who has always been there.

72

B is for **Bible**, where it says on day two,
God made the clean air for me and for you.
He divided the waters above and below;
Day three comes next, so there we shall go.

Notes For Parents and Teachers

The children need to understand that God made the world in six days and rested for one day. As well as teaching this from Genesis 1, read Exodus 20:11, which is the basis of the Fourth Commandment, and is one of the most important and easily understood reasons why God used six ordinary days to create the world. We read in Exodus 20:11 that God made everything in six days and rested for one day, which is the pattern for our seven-day week. Explain that if God had taken a million years for each day, then we would have a million-year rest, and our week would be seven million years long. Children will readily understand that this is obviously absurd.

Explain that on day one God made the space and the earth. The earth was covered with water (Genesis 1:1-5). On day two He put some water above the earth from the water on the earth (Genesis 1:6-8). You can explain that many creation scientists believe that this layer of water around the earth made it like a beautiful greenhouse, and sheltered it from harmful radiation. Teach them that this is probably one of the reasons why the people before Noah's flood lived to be hundreds of years old, and why even animals, such as dinosaurs, lived for a very long time.

Student Exercise

Discuss with the students the fact that there were day and night before the sun was created on day four. Have them read Genesis 1:3-5.

Tell them that light from one direction (implied by the phrase "evening and morning") is needed for day and night — but where did the light come from? They may have a lot of suggestions they could write down. Perhaps the light came from God, Himself (Revelation 21:23). The point of the exercise, however, is that we are not told where the light came from on days 1-3. God does not tell us everything — we can never know everything — otherwise we would be God. Make sure they understand that there will always be many questions we will not be able to answer, which is why we must have faith (Hebrews 11:6). However, the Christian faith is not without evidence. The Institute for Creation Research scientists have provided much scientific evidence that supports the Bible. Display some of their books and videos to the students if you have them.

75

C is for **Continent**, the first dry land,
Which God raised up by His powerful hand.
Then He commanded that all the plants grow;
The third day was truly a beautiful show.

Notes For Parents and Teachers

On day three God made the plants and the land surface, which rose out of the water. You can explain to them that some scholars have suggested there was only one large continent before the flood.

We read that on day three God made the plants "after his kind" (Genesis 1:11-12). This is the first occurrence of this phrase, which is repeated ten times in Genesis, Chapter 1. Emphasize that God made the plants and all the animals after their own kinds. This means that each group of animals and plants was made uniquely — they were not made from other kinds of animals or plants. Explain that this means that one kind of animal did not evolve into another, but that

God made different groups of animals and plants in the beginning, and that they stayed the same within their own groups. However, within a kind, there can be lots of variation (e.g., varieties of bears).

At this time it would also be good to talk again about the beauty of God's creation, and how a plant with a beautiful flower could not have happened just by chance. It had to have been made by the Creator — God.

Student Exercise

1. Have the students count the number of times the phrase "after his kind," or "after their kind" occurs in Genesis 1. (It appears a total of 10 times.)

2. Tell the students to draw a picture representing the earth before the flood. They can decide the shape and size of the land surface, etc. Some of them may want to draw this as one large continent, as some scholars have suggested. (If there were only one continent originally, it must have split up during the flood.) Have them mark a place where the Garden of Eden may have been, and the place where Noah may have lived and built the ark. They can also color this picture in — but tell them there were no deserts before the flood. The whole world would have been beautiful, with lots of green plants. Explain to them that the original world was destroyed by the flood, so the land surface today may be very different from that before the flood. Also, because of the flood, we do not know where the Garden of Eden was located.

D

is for **Dinosaur**, but you'll have to wait,
'Cause on day four other things God did make.
He formed the sun, the stars, and the moon.
Are you ready? We'll see those dinosaurs soon!

Notes For Parents and Teachers

On day four God made the sun, the moon, and the stars (Genesis 1:14-19). It is important to explain again that the sun was not created on day one. As a review question, ask, "How could we have day and night if there were no sun?" See if they remember previous discussions on this matter. Be sure they understand that God made light on day one, but that He didn't make the sun until day four, when it became the world's light-bearer from that time on.

Teach them that God made the sun, moon, and stars for signs and for seasons. Explain how we measure our month by the phases of the moon. You can also explain that people navigating ships, etc., use the stars to determine where they are on the earth. Also explain how the stars we can see change positions daily and according to the seasons of the earth, because of the earth's rotation on its axis as it revolves around the sun.

Student Exercise

Ask the students to write down how we determine the measurement for the following:

Day
Month
Year
Seven-day week

The students should know that the first three all come from astronomical observations (e.g., earth rotating on axis, earth and moon, earth and sun), but that the fourth has no basis other than the Bible. Hopefully, they remembered to quote Exodus 20:11, which tells us why God made everything in six days, and rested for one. The creation week is the only basis for our seven-day week.

E is for **Everything** that swims in the seas,
Made on day five, with the birds in the trees.
He also created the great Plesiosaur;
Reading God's Word, we can know this for sure.

Notes For Parents and Teachers

On day five God made the sea creatures and the birds (Genesis 1:20-23). This means He must have also made the great sea reptiles, like the plesiosaurs. Although the plesiosaur is not strictly a dinosaur (the word dinosaur specifically refers to land reptiles), according to evolutionists, they supposedly lived at the same time as the dinosaurs, and are often called marine dinosaurs. At this stage you could show them the picture from the dinosaur book, *The Great Dinosaur Mystery and the Bible*, page 47, which shows the dead animal pulled up by the nets of a Japanese fishing trawler in 1977. Some scientists were convinced the animal was a dead plesiosaur. If this really were a dead plesiosaur, then the idea that it lived millions of years ago obviously has some problems! (You can obtain this book in the USA from Master Books — phone 1-800-999-3777, or in Australia from Creation Science Foundation — phone: (07) 273 7650.)

Student Exercise

Ask the students to answer the following question in writing: "What came first, the chicken or the egg?" Then ask them to write down the reason for their answer.

The answer, of course, is that the chicken came first because God made the birds on day five, and then He told them to be fruitful and multiply (Genesis 1:22). Again, emphasize that the only way to know what came first is if someone were there to see the first chicken, or the first egg. Ask the question, "Who has always been there?" The answer, of course, is God. "Where do we go to find information concerning the creation of the world?" The Bible — God's Word. Through all of this you are training them to use the Bible as a foundation for their thinking — all their thinking must start with God's Word.

For the exceptionally bright student, you can explain that people who believe in evolution claim that life first evolved in the sea. However, God made the plants on day three, which means, according to the Bible, life first began on land, and not in the sea. Show them that, obviously, the story of evolution cannot be added to the Bible. It is totally different.

F is for **Fantastic** - that's all we can say,
As we see what God made on this, the sixth day!
Adam and Eve, and the pouched kangaroo;
The rest of the animals, and dinosaurs, too.

Notes For Parents and Teachers

On day six the Bible tells us that God made all the land creatures, and the first two people, Adam and Eve. If He made all the land creatures on this day, then He must have made animals like kangaroos, bears, horses, etc., as well as dinosaurs, because dinosaurs were also land creatures. Explain that the word "dinosaur" was invented by a man named Sir Richard Owen (a famous British anatomist) in 1841, to describe the bones of great reptiles that had been found in the earth. The word dinosaur means "terrible lizard." This is why the word dinosaur does not appear in the Bible — it is a made-up word, invented in 1841.

Make sure they understand that by reading the Bible we can be sure that dinosaurs and people lived at the same time, because each of the days of creation was an ordinary day, and God made Adam and Eve on the same day He made the land animals. Explain to them that those who believe in evolution think dinosaurs lived millions of years before man even appeared on the earth. Obviously, the story from the Bible is very different from the theory of evolution.

Student Exercise

Have the students exercise their creativity by composing a four-line poem to illustrate that Adam and Eve lived beside dinosaurs. These could be printed on poster board and put up around the room.

You could use this example:

God made dinosaurs on day six;
With Adam and Eve they all did mix.
He put them all in a garden to live;
To God our praises we surely must give.

G is for the **Garden** God specially made,
Where Adam and Eve
could always have stayed.
Living in Eden, a world without sin;
What a beautiful place for them to live in!

Notes For Parents and Teachers

When God made Adam and Eve, He made a beautiful garden for them, in which to live. You can read this in Genesis 2. Explain to the children that in this garden God placed two very special trees: the tree of knowledge of good and evil, and the tree of life (Genesis 2:8-9). Adam was told that they were not to eat of the tree of knowledge of good and evil. God gave them this rule, which He wanted them to obey (Genesis 2:16-17).

Make sure they understand that this was a very beautiful place. It was a perfect world where everything was in total harmony. Get them to picture in their minds a beautiful rain forest where there are lots of green plants, lush vegetation, beautiful big trees, beautiful ponds and water lilies, and creeks with crystal-clear water flowing. Then tell them that the Garden of Eden would have been a much more beautiful place than even this.

Student Exercise

Ask the students this question: "Why did the fish obey God and swallow Jonah?" The answer, of course, is that because God made the fish in the first place, it had to obey God. Get the students to write down other examples in the Bible where animals or the elements obeyed God's Word (e.g., the ravens feeding Elijah, the wind and the sea calming at Jesus' Word, etc.). There are many examples.

After you have gone through all the examples (add more yourself if the students could not think of many), ask them, "Why did _____ obey God?" They should give the same answer each time: "Because He made it." Then ask the question, "Why do you have to obey God?" Answer: "Because He made me." Then you can use this to talk about being obedient to God's Word — and thus to their parents and teachers. Discuss the Ten Commandments — have them read Exodus, Chapter 20.

H

is for **Hungry**, it's how we describe
A big dinosaur with his mouth open wide.
Adam wasn't scared to watch dinosaurs eat,
Because all the creatures ate plants, and not meat.

Notes For Parents and Teachers

Most children think of dinosaurs as being very large. Certainly, the bones we have found show some of them as being very large, but many of them were very small — some as small as chickens. Suggest to them that Adam would not have been frightened of a huge, hungry dinosaur with a big mouth, because the Bible tells us that when God first made the animals, and Adam and Eve, they ate only plants (Genesis 1:29-30). Even the biggest dinosaur would have eaten only plants. Thus, Adam would not have been frightened of a dinosaur with a big mouth opened wide, ready to eat. He knew that the dinosaur would not have wanted to eat him, because originally, animals did not eat meat; and Adam would not have wanted to eat a dinosaur because Adam and Eve were also told to eat only plants and fruits.

Some children may wonder why animals have sharp teeth if they were not created to eat meat. There are many possible answers to this, and we suggest that you obtain *The Answers Book*, by Ken Ham, Andrew Snelling, and Carl Wieland, which has a detailed answer suggesting a number of solutions. (Obtain this book in the USA from Master Books — phone 1-800-999-3777, and in Australia from Creation Science Foundation — phone (07) 273 7650.) However, you can explain to them that their mothers use sharp knives to cut up vegetables, and so animals would have needed sharp teeth just to cut through vegetables and fruits that they were eating. In other words, just because an animal has sharp teeth does not mean it eats meat. It simply means it has sharp teeth for eating other types of foods!

Student Exercise

Take the students to the library and look up books on animals. Try to find animals that have real sharp teeth but that eat only (or mainly) plants. (Hint: look at the panda, some of the bears, certain monkeys, lizards, etc.) The students could do a written project on the information they collect.

I is the letter in the middle of s**I**n,
To remind us all of the trouble we're in.
Dinosaurs, people, and the whole universe;
Because of man's sin, God judged with a curse.

Notes For Parents and Teachers

Tell the children that in this beautiful garden, Adam and Eve disobeyed God and ate some fruit from the tree of knowledge of good and evil because the devil tempted them (Genesis 3:1-7). Explain how wrong it was to yield to that temptation and disobey God.

Because of this rebellion — not obeying God's rules — sin came into the world (Romans 5:12). Clearly define sin to them. It is disobedience or rebellion against God's rules. Explain to them that all of us have the problem of wanting to disobey God at times, and that this is why we often don't want to obey our teachers, or our parents, or our employers and supervisors. We have in us this rebellion against authority because we are all descendants of Adam; consequently we don't always want to obey God's rules.

Teach them that because of this rebellion, God placed a curse on the world — in fact, on the whole universe (Genesis 3:14-19). Romans 8:20-22 tells us that the whole of creation is groaning and travailing in pain because of Adam's sin.

Romans 5:12 says that death came into the world because of Adam's sin. The fact that they see animals eating other animals today, or even that some of the dinosaurs ate other animals, was not a part of the original creation before sin, because the animals originally ate only plants. However, because of sin, God allowed death to come into the world; therefore, some of the animals would have started eating other animals, and perhaps even people. It is also important to understand that there would not have been dead dinosaurs (bones of dinosaurs — fossils) before Adam sinned. This is one major reason why Christians can't really believe in both evolution and the Bible.

You can use this section to emphasize to them how awful sin is, and that all the terrible things we see in the world — the death and suffering — are because of this sin which we inherited from our great, great, great … granddaddy — Adam. Explain that God had to judge sin because God is holy and perfect. The very reason God used death is so that once again we will be able to live in a perfect world after we die, or when Jesus comes again. Tell them that without death, we could not go to live with God; we would always be separated from God. How terrible this would be! This will be discussed further when we get to the letter "U."

We can assume that some of the dinosaurs, because of sin, started eating animals — even other dinosaurs. Read Genesis 9: 1-3. This was told to Noah after the flood. Thus man, for the FIRST time since the creation, was told that he could eat meat. Originally he, like the animals, ate only plants.

Student Exercise

List all the things you can think of that you eat now, that man would not have been able to eat before Genesis 9, if he had been obedient to God (e.g., pork sausage, bacon, ham — any animal product).

88

J means **Just** awful - I'm sure we could say
The effects of sin grew worse every day.
Flesh became violent, the Bible reveals.
Were people and creatures now dinosaur meals?

Notes For Parents and Teachers

Read to the children the passage from Genesis 6:12-13, which states that all flesh had become corrupt (violent). Again, explain that this was because sin had entered the world, and so God had cursed the world.

Because the Bible says "ALL" flesh had become violent, you can tell them that it wasn't just people who became violent, but animals, also. Thus, dinosaurs, as well as other animals, probably became violent, and started killing each other and killing people.

God must have been very sad to see how violent His beautiful world had become. Remember how it once was? Now it was becoming a very terrible place in which to live.

Student Exercise

Have the students pretend they are newspaper reporters at the time of Noah. Ask them to write a short article on what they saw happening in the world — how wicked it had become. Have them make up a headline for this article.

Using poster board, or something similar, make up the front page of a newspaper and call it "The Daily Curse." Paste a number of the students' articles on this page and put the poster up on the wall as a reminder of how wicked the world was in Noah's day. You may want to develop several newspapers and give them different names.

**K** is for **Knowledge**, which made Noah sad;
The world would be judged,
because people were bad!
God warned He would send a terrible flood
That would cover the world with water and mud.

Notes For Parents and Teachers

Read Genesis 6:8 and share with them the fact that there was only one righteous man in the whole world — Noah. He was the only man who loved God, and had not turned against Him. Because the world had become so wicked, God warned this righteous man, Noah, that He was going to send a flood to destroy the world.

Tell them how faithful Noah was. He did everything God commanded him to do (Genesis 6:22). Because Noah was such a good man and loved God, God promised to save him, his three sons, and their wives, from this flood that was going to cover the whole world, and which would destroy all the wicked people and violent animals.

You can also point out to them that the majority of people (in fact, nearly everyone in the world) was wrong. Today, because most scientists don't believe in creation, people say they must be right. However, the majority may not always be right. In Noah's day the majority was wrong.

Student Exercise

The students can pretend they are Noah, before the flood. Have them make up a one-minute sermon that Noah might have preached to warn the people about the impending flood. They can write out this sermon and then stand up in front of the other students (pretend they are the wicked people), and preach the sermon to them.

L

L is for **Listen**: Noah knew that he should,
As soon as God said, "Make an ark out of wood.
Take each land animal, two-by-two;
Your family will be the hard-working crew."

Notes For Parents and Teachers

Read to them Genesis 6:14, where God told Noah to build a big boat to save his family, and representatives of all the kinds of air-breathing land animals, from the flood. This boat was to be made of wood, and God would send two of each land animal onto this boat, or ark. In some cases, He would send seven of each kind.

Ask them what happened to the animals that didn't go on the ark. If the world were covered with water, obviously, they drowned.

If Noah's flood did occur, you would expect to find billions of dead things, buried in rock layers, laid down by water all over the earth. Tell them that's exactly what we find.

Because of Noah's flood, there would have been lots of mud all over the earth, and it would have buried many of the animals and plants. We find their remains in these layers, all over the earth. This fits with the fact that animals could die only after Adam sinned. These fossils of animals could not have formed until after the fall. For fossils to form, there needs to be lots of water and mud. Thus, the flood provided an excellent mechanism for forming literally millions of fossils after Adam sinned. (At this stage you may like to read them the book *What Really Happened to the Dinosaurs*, by Ken Ham and John Morris. This can be obtained in the USA from Master Books — phone 1-800-999-3777, and in Australia, from Creation Science Foundation — phone (07) 273-7650.)

Read the passage from Genesis 7:2-3, where God said He would send two of EVERY kind of air-breathing land animal on board the ark. Genesis 6:19 tells us that God would send a male and female of each kind. (There were to be seven each of the clean beasts and fowls, and only two each of the unclean animals.)

If God sent every kind of animal on the ark, this would have included dinosaurs. God made no exceptions; therefore, dinosaurs must have gone on the ark as well.

Student Exercise

Have the students write the caption, "billions of dead things, buried in rock layers, laid down by water all over the earth" on a poster. They can then illustrate this caption on the poster. Get them to memorize the caption and recite it.

M is for **Monster**, like the great dinosaur;
But how could he enter the ark through the door?
Well, many dinosaurs were really quite small;
The young ones, especially, were not very tall.

Notes For Parents and Teachers

Because most children (and even adults) think of dinosaurs as extremely large creatures, they have trouble visualizing how they could fit into the ark. Explain to them that some reptiles have been observed to continue to grow as long as they live. Because dinosaurs probably were reptiles, maybe some of them also would have continued to grow all their life. However, explain that even the largest dinosaur was very small when it hatched out of an egg. It may have taken a long time, perhaps hundreds of years, for these dinosaurs to reach their enormous sizes.

Because God selected the animals to send to Noah, no doubt he would have selected young, healthy animals, ready for the new world after the flood. God would not have selected a large dinosaur to go in the ark, but probably a young adult. In the famous book *The Genesis Flood*, by Dr.'s Henry Morris and John Whitcomb, they estimate, assuming the average size of an animal to be the size of a sheep, that no more than seventy thousand individual animals were needed on the ark to represent all the kinds of land animals (including extinct animals); this would have filled only half of the ark's space. There was plenty of room on the ark! There was even room for more people, if they had believed Noah and asked to be saved from the flood. But, sadly, they did not do that. This book is available in the USA from Master Books — phone 1-800-999-3777, and in Australia from Creation Science Foundation — phone (07) 273 7650.

Again, remind them that some dinosaurs were as small as chickens.

Student Exercise

Give the students a library research assignment. Have them look up the names of as many varieties of domestic dogs as possible. Also get them to look up the different types of wolves, and to look up pictures of coyotes and dingos, and write all these names on a list. Explain to them that these animals are all dogs, and came from an original dog kind that may have looked like a wolf. You may be able to get a local dog breeder to tell the students how many different varieties of dogs have been bred over the past hundred years. Thus, use dogs as a way of explaining variation within a group of animals. Use the domestic dogs, dingos, and wolves as examples of the same kind, but with variation in shape, size, weight, etc. Explain that this type of situation would be true of all other groups of animals.

Have the students find a book which lists the hundreds of dinosaur names. Show them that the reconstructions they see can be organized into groups that look similar. Explain that although there are hundreds of names of dinosaurs, there may actually have been as few as fifty different KINDS. Just as there is great variation within the dog KIND, so there could have been great variation within the different dinosaur KINDS.

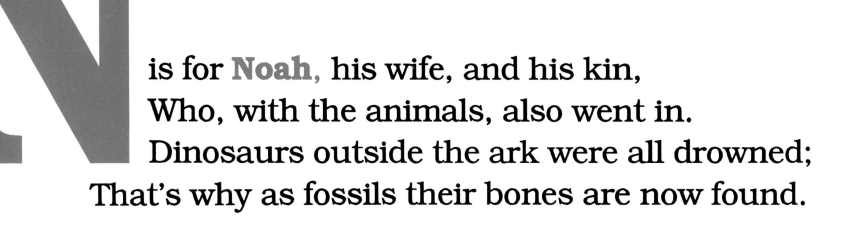

N is for **Noah**, his wife, and his kin,
Who, with the animals, also went in.
Dinosaurs outside the ark were all drowned;
That's why as fossils their bones are now found.

Notes For Parents and Teachers

Because of the effect of the flood, we find plants and animals buried in mud all over the earth. At the end of the flood, these mud layers eventually hardened and turned to stone. The preserved remains of animals and plants found in these rocks are called fossils.

Share with them the fact that, probably, most of the fossils on the earth's surface would have been formed because of the effect of this worldwide flood. Also explain to them that if you add up the dates in the Bible, this flood occurred only about four-and-a-half-thousand years ago, which would mean that most of the fossils, including dinosaur fossils, would be no more than about 4,500 years of age.

Student Exercise

Get the students to obtain a glass bottle and half fill it with dirt. Then have them fill the rest of the bottle with water, and shake furiously (after putting a lid on the bottle, or putting their hand over the end as they shake it). Then have them put the bottle down, and let the water and mud settle. Have them observe that, as the mud settles, it forms different layers. Have them draw a diagram of these layers.

Show them a picture of the Grand Canyon. Ask them to draw a diagram of the Grand Canyon layers on a large piece of paper. Then have them put the following caption on their diagram:

Lots of water and lots of mud,
Formed these layers during Noah's flood.

Explain to them that if the little bit of water and dirt in their bottle formed into layers after mixing it up, you would expect to find lots of layers all over the earth, if the flood of Noah's day mixed up lots of mud.

O is for **Out** of the ark they all ran,
   Once the huge vessel came safely to land.
Stegasaurs, lambeosaurs, nodosaurs, and more;
After the flood there were dinosaurs galore!

Notes For Parents and Teachers

If dinosaurs went on the ark, then they must have come out of the ark after the flood. This would mean that dinosaurs lived in the world after the flood.

Review with the children the fact that dinosaurs were created on the same day as Adam. Provided they hadn't died out (which is unlikely, particularly in the light of Job 40, and dragon legends as discussed in "S" and "T"), they lived at the same time as Noah, they went into the ark, and they came off the ark after the flood.

Also remind them that Noah's ark rested on a mountain for a number of months before the animals came out, so there was plenty of time for the mud to harden and for plants to grow, which would have provided food for the dinosaurs after this terrible event.

Student Exercise

Have the students pretend they are Noah keeping a diary during his adventure on the ark. Have them call it "The Ark Log." Get them to choose five days — either at the beginning, the middle, or near the end of the voyage — and write an entry for each day.

P is for **Pronounce**: are the names hard for you? Iguanodon, diplodocus, now how did you do? Brachiosaurus, tyrannosaurus, and others as well; What happened to them is the story we'll tell.

Notes For Parents and Teachers

One of the things you can do here is to obtain Dr. Duane Gish's book *Dinosaurs: Those Terrible Lizards*. This was the first major creationist book on dinosaurs. Either read the book to them, or select a number of different dinosaur names and teach the children to pronounce them. Suggest to them that these dinosaurs would have been living in the present world after the flood. In the USA, this book can be obtained from Master Books — phone 1-800-999-3777, and in Australia from Creation Science Foundation — phone (07) 273 7650.

Student Exercise

Have each of the students learn ten of their favorite dinosaur names. Then see how fast they can say all 10 names. Perhaps you could have a competition, and time each person as they say the ten names.

It can be fun learning dinosaur names and how to pronounce them.

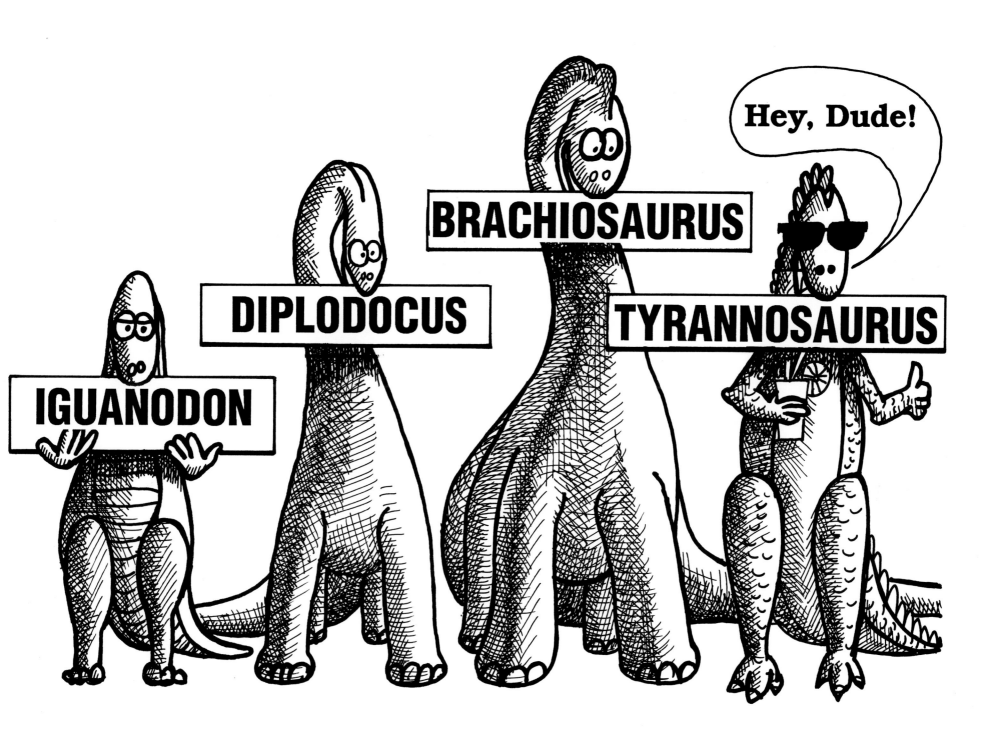

Q is for **Question** - why can't we any more,
Look around and see even one dinosaur?
They're surely all dead, it's as simple as that;
Try to guess why - put on your thinking hat.

Notes For Parents and Teachers

Obviously, if dinosaurs came off the ark, they must have lived in the world after the flood. However, we don't see any today, so they must have died out. If there were at least fifty kinds of dinosaurs represented on the ark, then presumably at least fifty kinds of dinosaurs lived after the flood.

Student Exercise

Ask the students for suggestions as to why they think the dinosaurs must have disappeared. We don't seem to see them around us today, and unless they're living in jungles where we haven't found them, we don't believe they are living at all in this present world. However, they did come out of the ark, and they were living on this earth only thousands of years ago. Help them come up with ideas as to what they think happened to the dinosaurs, and get them to write down all of these suggestions.

R is for **Reasons** - perhaps there are more.
After the flood, times were tougher for sure:
Volcanoes and storms,
then drought and snow,
Maybe people killed them - they frightened them so.

Notes For Parents and Teachers

Tell them that dinosaurs would have laid eggs, and produced more dinosaurs, so there would have been an increasing number of dinosaurs after the flood. However, explain to them that after the flood, the world was not a perfect place. There would have been local floods, and drought, and snow, and people probably would have become violent again, because all human beings suffer from the same problem that Adam brought into the world — sin.

Review again all the reasons the students came up with that may have caused dinosaurs to eventually die out. Also share with them that after the flood there was probably an Ice Age. This may be alluded to in Job 38:29. Because dinosaurs were probably reptiles, they might not have coped very well in a cold climate, so this also may have contributed to killing them off.

Student Exercise

One of the reasons the students might come up with in regard to the extinction of the dinosaurs, would be that people killed them. As a fun exercise, have the students imagine they owned a restaurant while dinosaurs were still alive, and all the items on the menu had to come from dinosaurs. Get them to develop a breakfast, lunch, and dinner menu, and make up a name for the restaurant.

Some ideas:

Breakfast: Dino One-Egg Omlette — suitable for 20 people.

Lunch: Tyrannosaurus Drumstick — need 5 hours to eat.

Dinner: Bronto Burger.

S is for the Story from God's Holy Book,
About a great beast;
when he walked, the ground shook.
Behemoth, or monster, was this animal's name;
Our word "dinosaur" means almost the same.

Notes For Parents and Teachers

If dinosaurs went on the ark, and came off the ark, and were created by God on day six, then are they mentioned in the Bible?

At this time, read Job 40:15-24, and consider the description of a great monster called "behemoth." The Bible describes it as being "chief of the ways of God," and so it must have been the largest land animal God created. Show them that this description fits a dinosaur, such as a brachiosaurus, or supersaurus, or seismosaurus, or some other great dinosaur. The description says this animal had a tail like a cedar tree. Show them that a description like this does not fit an elephant or a hippopotamus, but that it does fit a dinosaur. Actually, there is a special Hebrew word for elephant, and also for hippopotamus. The word "behemoth" literally means "great quadruped." This means it was a great animal on four legs. Job 40:19 says this animal was "chief of the ways of God," which probably means it was the largest land animal God made — thus it had to be a dinosaur. Tell them that in this passage from Job, God is talking to Job

about this creature. Job was a man who lived after the flood, and obviously knew about dinosaurs. The Bible thus tells us that dinosaurs lived after the flood, and that once again they lived at the same time as people. ICR has printed a beautiful color poster of "behemoth" alongside Job, with a Bible verse from Job about this creature. You can purchase this unique poster in the USA from ICR — phone (619) 448 0900, or in Australia from Creation Science Foundation — phone (07) 273 7650. This would make a great wall poster for your home, school, or church.

Student Exercise

If some dinosaurs grew so large before the flood because animals (and people) lived for a long time (hundreds of years — see Genesis 5:5), why did "behemoth" grow so large after the flood, since we know people in today's world live to be only seventy years or so?

Have the students read the following verses to see if they can find a possible answer: Genesis 9:28-29, Genesis 11:10-11, Genesis 11:13, Genesis 11:17, Genesis

11:19, Genesis 11:21, Genesis 11:25, Genesis 11:32.

If the students read through Genesis Chapters 9-11, they will learn that people still lived for hundreds of years immediately after the flood, but then their life span started to shorten dramatically. Perhaps some dinosaurs lived for hundreds of years immediately after the flood, and thus may still have grown very large — e.g., "behemoth." However, have them do library research to find out which animal is the largest ever known to have lived on earth. They will discover it is the blue whale, which still lives in the oceans today. It does not live for hundreds of years — but it is the largest known animal to have ever existed. Thus, have the students realize that it may not have been the dinosaurs' length of life that enabled them to grow to enormous sizes. It may have just simply been a characteristic that God built into their genes. Help them to understand there is still much information about dinosaurs that is unknown, and so we have to be very tentative in regard to many of the things we say about them. (After all, we were not there to see them living.)

T is for **Tales** that we often hear
About terrible dragons that made men fear.
Maybe these tales could actually be
Stories of dinosaurs men used to see.

Notes For Parents and Teachers

Ask the students if they have ever heard any dragon legends. There are many legends around the world that say there used to be dragons, and that people killed them. (See *The Great Dinosaur Mystery and the Bible*, mentioned earlier.) Ask them for descriptions of what these dragons were like. Show them that many of these descriptions actually could fit dinosaurs.

Some of these dragon legends talk of "fire-breathing dragons." Could some of the dinosaurs have "breathed fire"? Refer to page 50 in Dr. Gish's book *Dinosaurs: Those Terrible Lizards*, mentioned earlier.

Suggest to them that perhaps these dragon legends are based on real encounters with large animals that people called dragons, but which were actually dinosaurs. People may have embellished these stories over the years. Thus there may be evidence from all around that dinosaurs lived in different parts of the world, alongside people.

Student Exercise

Write a 20-word message about sighting a big animal. Have the children sit down together. Whisper the message to the first person, and have them whisper it to the next person and so on. Then have the last person say out loud the message that they received. It will most likely have some similarities to the original message, but it will also have many differences. Explain how stories can change when handed down by word of mouth — people forget some things, and add other things; thus, the dragon legends could be variations of true stories with some elements of the original versions, but now containing many differences, also.

Now write out a different message. Have the first student copy exactly what you have written, and then have the next child copy from this one and so on. Get the last student to read the final copy — it should be the same as the original, if they all copied it exactly. Explain that the Bible has been handed down in written form from the beginning (even Adam probably wrote down parts of Genesis which Moses used to compile the book — Genesis 5:1). Also, God supernaturally watched over the people who copied the manuscripts (II Timothy 3:16; II Peter 1:21). When something is handed down in written form, the possibility of error is greatly reduced compared to the problems in things handed down orally. The students probably made some mistakes even when copying, because they are FALLIBLE beings. However, help them understand that the Bible has been supernaturally preserved by the INFALLIBLE Creator God.

U

is for **Understand**, which we want to do;
The Bible explains the dinosaurs for you.
It also tells how from sin to be saved;
By trusting in Jesus, who rose from the grave.

Notes For Parents and Teachers

Reinforce the fact that when we start with the Word of God — the God who knows everything because He was always there — we can understand about dinosaurs. However, share with them that the Bible not only tells us about dinosaurs, it also tells us about ourselves and the trouble we're in because of sin (Romans 3:23; I Corinthians 15:22, Isaiah 64:6, John 3:3-5).

Read to them from Matthew 27:27-31, and 28:1-7, and tell them about the fact that because of sin, the one who created the world (Colossians 1:16), came to earth and died on a cross, and was raised from the dead so we can spend eternity with God, and thus live with Him in a perfect place.

Explain to them that this is why God judged the world with death. Someone who was perfect needed to die to atone for our sin. The only one who could do this was God, Himself, because He is sinless, and is our Creator. He sent His Son, the Lord Jesus Christ, to die and be raised from the dead so that our sins could be forgiven, and so that we could spend eternity with the Lord Jesus. Explain the whole of the Gospel message at this stage, from creation to redemption.

Student Exercise

Have the students collect funeral notices from their local newspaper for a week. At the end of this time, collect all the notices and summarize the sex, age, and occupations of those who had died. Ask the students what they can learn from this.

They should realize that death could come at any time for anyone. No one is exempt. It doesn't matter whether you are male or female, young or old, famous or not — no one is immune from death.

Ask the students what they should do, now that they know this. The answer should be to BE READY — to be sure that if they died today, they would go to be with the Creator, because they have been born again as the Scripture says they must be.

V

V is for how **Very** much we can say
We all should read the Bible each day.
Dinosaurs, we've proven, are no mystery;
God's Word teaches us true history.

Notes For Parents and Teachers

Read the children the following passages: Psalm 1:2, Joshua 1:8, II Timothy 2:15. These verses tell us that we should read God's Word every day. Read Psalm 119:11 — this tells us we should memorize God's Word. Explain how important that is; that, just as we need to eat good food to be physically healthy, so we need to "eat" God's food, the Bible, to be spiritually healthy.

If we read God's Word every day, we will not be led astray by people who try to tell us that His Word is false — who tell us evolution is true, and that dinosaurs lived millions of years ago.

Tell them that the evolutionists do not know anyone who has always been there, or who knows everything. But we have the Word of God — the God Who has always been there, and Who knows everything. We can know what is right about the history of this world, about who we are, why we are here, and where we are going.

Student Exercise

Have the students construct a "My Bible Diet" poster. For example:

My Bible Diet, by Johnny Smith.

1. Read my Bible morning and night.
2. Think about what I have read.
3. Memorize verses every day.

Also, have them put some of the above Bible verses on the poster.

W is for **Watchfulness**,
which we should all learn,
Since some day Jesus, our Lord, will return.
He's going to judge this world once again;
But this time by fire, instead of by rain.

Notes For Parents and Teachers

Read the following passages to the children: Acts 1:9-11, Revelation 1:7, I Thessalonians 4:16-18. These passages tell us that Jesus Christ, who came to earth to die for our sin, is coming back some day. Explain to them that this world was judged once by water, but that next time it is going to be judged by fire (II Peter 3:10).

Again, refer back to the story of the flood, and show how the people who did not trust God's Word were destroyed at the time of the flood, but that those who did trust God's Word were saved on the ark (Genesis 7:23).

Share with them the wonderful fact that if they trust God's Word today, the Lord Jesus will save them from the judgment which is coming on this earth. Tell them how much we need to be like Noah, who trusted God's Word. If we do this, God will save us from the judgment to come.

Also, at this time, remind them of the story of the rainbow. In Genesis 9:12-13, God tells us that He put a rainbow in the sky as a sign that He will never again send a worldwide flood.

Tell them that the next time they see a rainbow, it should remind them that God once judged the world with water, but that He will never do it again. This should be a warning that He will next judge the world by fire, but that if we are trusting in Him, as did Noah, we will be saved from this judgment of fire, just as Noah was saved from the judgment of the flood.

Student Exercise

Have them write down the 7 major colors of the rainbow — red, orange, yellow, green, blue, indigo, violet. Write the word rainbow as follows:

R
A
I
N
B
O
W

Beside each letter, put a color of the rainbow, beginning with Red. (The only reason for this part is to give them something to do and make their page look colorful!) Then opposite the color, get them to write a word for each letter and use all seven words to tell some of the things they have learned in this book. For example:

R — Ready — Be ready for Jesus when He comes back.
A — Answers — The Bible has the answers about life.
I — Into — Dinosaurs went into the Ark.
N — No — No people outside the Ark survived the flood.
B — Behemoth — A dinosaur that lived beside Job.
O — Out — Out of the Ark dinosaurs came.
W — Water — Water covered the whole earth during the Flood.

116

The
BIG BANG
is
definitely
coming!

X is in eXcited, which Christians should be,
One day we know that heaven we'll see.
There'll be no more dying, or crying or pain;
For God, our Creator, forever will reign.

Notes For Parents and Teachers

Read Revelation 21:1-5, and Revelation 22: 1-5. These passages tell us there is a time coming when there will be no more death or suffering. The death and suffering that exist in the world today are because of sin. When we dig up the bones of animals such as dinosaurs, it should remind us that death is in the world because of sin.

One day God is going to judge this world, and make it into a perfect place again, where there will be no more death, and where we will be able to sing praises to our Creator. However, those who don't trust in the Lord Jesus Christ will be separated from God, and will suffer for the rest of eternity.

Student Exercise

Conduct a class discussion. Have the children try to list all the jobs that people have now that will not be needed in heaven. For example: doctor, policeman, fireman, nurses, etc. Really, the conclusion to which they will come is that heaven will be TOTALLY different from what we are used to now. Discuss with them what it might be like, and the famous Christians whom we will meet. Help them to understand that heaven is a REAL place with REAL people, and those who are Christians WILL be going there someday.

Have them looking forward to heaven!

119

Y

Y is for **Years**; how long could it be,
Since God made the world for you and for me?
"Probably only six thousand or so,"
Say many good scientists; they ought to know!

Notes For Parents and Teachers

Emphasize to the children that when we add up all the dates in the Bible, from the first day of creation through the flood, and right up until the present time, it amounts to only about six thousand years. Share with them how different this is from the evolutionary scientists who say that dinosaurs lived millions of years ago. Remind them that no scientist was there, but that God has always been there, and that God's Word tells us the truth about dinosaurs and about history.

Tell them that there are many scientists who do not believe in evolution and millions of years. These are special scientists called creation scientists, and they work in many research laboratories around the world. Some of them work at the Institute for Creation Research in the USA. Tell them they are highly qualified scientists who have done a lot of research to show that the world is only thousands of years old, just as the Bible tells us.

Student Exercise

Obtain the book **Men of Science: Men of God**. This is available in the USA from Master Books — phone 1-800-999-3777, and in Australia from Creation Science Foundation — phone (07) 273-7650. This book lists many of the scientists of the past who were very famous, and who were also creationists (e.g., Newton, Kepler, Faraday, etc.).

Make up sets of six different cards, each about the size of a business card. At the top of each card print, "Adopt a Scientist." Then select six different scientists from the list in **Men of Science: Men of God**, and write their names, when they lived, and what they were famous for on the card. (You could also have the students make these cards — only larger.)

Tell the students to carry the cards around for a week, and memorize the information on them. At the end of the week they should be able to recite the names of six famous scientists who believed in creation. Give them a test!

Z

Z is for the **Zeal** which people should see,
As we tell the truth about history.
The dinosaurs certainly have not evolved;
Through God's Holy Word, the puzzle is solved!

Notes For Parents and Teachers

Read the passage of the Great Commission from Mark 16:15, which says that we should go all over the world telling people about the Gospel message. This message tells us that God created a perfect world, sin entered the world, and that death came as a result of sin. But, Jesus Christ came and died for our sin, and one day He's coming back to remake this world.

Because we know the truth about history, we can tell people that God made the world. We need to oppose the wrong ideas people have, such as evolution, which keep them from believing the Bible.

Many people mistakenly believe that dinosaurs lived millions of years ago, and that, because this is in opposition to what God's Word teaches, we can't trust the Bible. We need to tell them the truth about dinosaurs, and that we have the answers about where they came from, and what happened to them, because we have God's Holy Word — the Word of the one who knows everything, who has always been there, who made us, who also died for us, and who is coming back to restore this world to a beautiful place (Acts 3:21).

Student Exercise

Write out a commitment letter that each student could complete and take home to show family and friends. Perhaps you could have this done on special paper in special hand writing. The following is just a suggestion on how to word such a letter:

I, _____ (name), hereby declare that I am going to live with Jesus _____ (forever), because I have _____ (repented) of my sin, which I inherited from _____(Adam).

I, _____ (name), also declare that I love the Lord Jesus with all my _____ (heart) and _____ (soul).

I, _____ (name), know this is true because Jesus died for my _____ (sin), and conquered death because He _____ (rose) from the dead.

I, _____ (name), know this because the _____ (Bible) tells me.

I, _____ (name), declare that I am a Christian.

Signed _____ Date _____

122

123

NOTES